EARNING, SAVING, SPENDING

Credit Cards and Debit Cards

Margaret Hall

Heinemann
LIBRARY

www.heinemannlibrary.co.uk
Visit our website to find out more information about Heinemann Library books.

To order:
☎ Phone +44 (0) 1865 888066
🖹 Fax +44 (0) 1865 314091
🖥 Visit www.heinemannlibrary.co.uk

Heinemann Library is an imprint of Capstone Global Library Limited, a company incorporated in England and Wales having its registered office at 7 Pilgrim Street, London, EC4V 6LB – Registered company number: 6695582

Heinemann is a registered trademark of Pearson Education Limited, under licence to Capstone Global Library Limited

Text © Capstone Global Library Limited 2009
First published in hardback in 2009
Paperback edition first published in 2010

Edited by Charlotte Guillain and Catherine Veitch
Designed by Kim Miracle, Victoria Bevan and
   AMR Design Ltd
Illustrated by Mark Preston
Picture research by Hannah Taylor
Production: Victoria Fitzgerald

Originated by Dot Gradations Ltd
Printed and bound in China by Leo Paper
   Products Ltd

ISBN 978 0 4311 1680 8 (hardback)
13 12 11 10 09
10 9 8 7 6 5 4 3 2 1

ISBN 978 0 4311 1685 3 (paperback)
14 13 12 11 10
10 9 8 7 6 5 4 3 2 1

British Library Cataloguing in Publication Data
Hall, Margaret
Credit cards and debit cards. - 2nd ed.
(Earning, saving, spending)
332.7'6
A full catalogue record for this book is available from the British Library.

Acknowledgements
We would like to thank the following for permission to reproduce photographs: © Alamy pp. **4** (John Powell Photographer), **21** (Chris Rout), **22** (Jack Sparticus), **23** (David J. Green), **26** (John James), **27** (Bubbles); © AlamySuperstock p. **29**; © Getty Images pp. **17** (PM Images), **28** (PBJ Images); © Pearson Education Ltd/Tudor Photography pp. **7**, **13**, **25**; © Wishlist Images 2008 pp. **6**, **14**, **15**, **18**, **24** (Harry Rhodes).

Cover photograph of adult punching buttons on credit card reader reproduced with permission of © Masterfile.

Every effort has been made to contact copyright holders of material reproduced in this book. Any omissions will be rectified in subsequent printings if notice is given to the publishers.

Contents

Some words are shown in bold, **like this**. You can find out what they mean by looking in the glossary on page 30.

Spending without cash

Banks offer **services** to their customers that let them buy things without using **cash**. These services include **cheques** and special **bank cards**. A cheque is like a note telling the bank to pay money to someone. Bank cards are thin, plastic cards. They can be used in many places.

Most shops let customers use bank cards to buy items.

In some ways, it is safer to use a bank card to buy things. If cash gets lost or stolen, anyone can use it. A bank card has the owner's name on it and his or her signature. It also has a secret number called a **personal identification number (PIN)** that only the owner knows. This means that only the person who owns the card should be able to use it.

These bank cards look quite different but they all work in the same way.

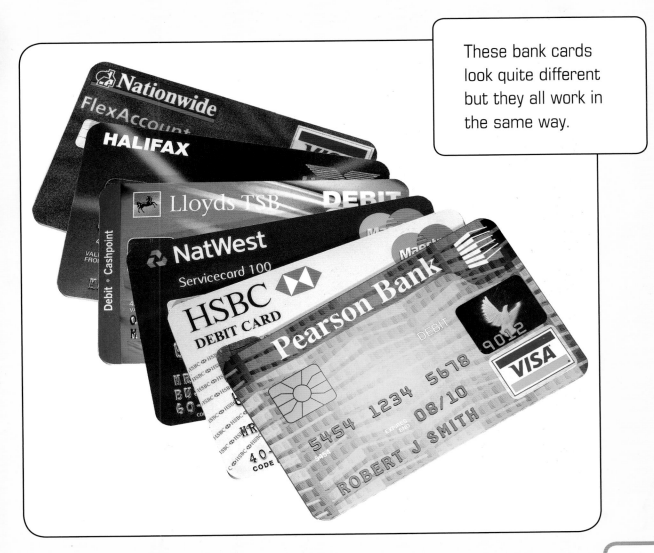

Opening a current account

To pay for things without cash, people need to open a **current account**. To open a current account, the customer gives the bank some money. This is called a **deposit**.

Banks offer different types of current account.

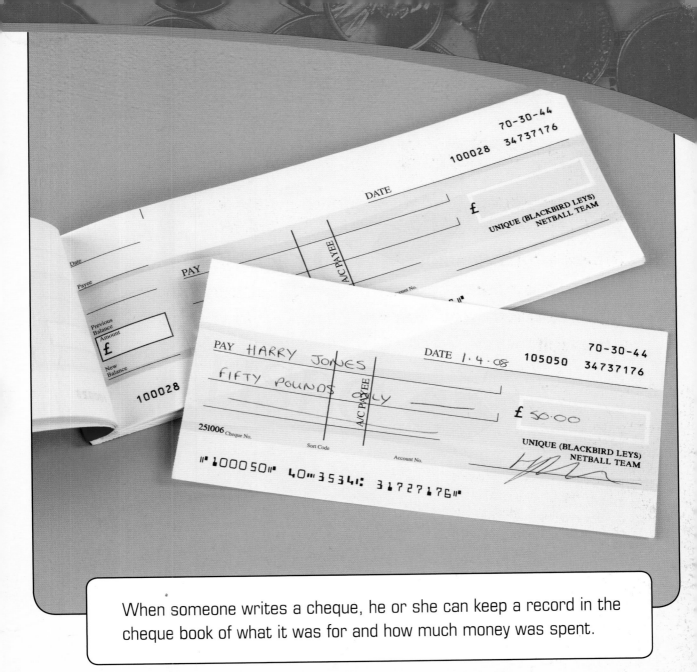

70-30-44
100028   34737176

DATE

£

UNIQUE (BLACKBIRD LEYS)
NETBALL TEAM

A/C PAYEE

Date

Payee   PAY

Previous
Balance
Amount
£

New
Balance

100028

PAY HARRY JONES   DATE 1.4.08   105050   70-30-44
34737176

FIFTY POUNDS ONLY

A/C PAYEE

£ 50.00

UNIQUE (BLACKBIRD LEYS)
NETBALL TEAM

251006 Cheque No.   Sort Code   Account No.

⑈⑈ 100050⑈⑈ 40⑈3534⑈: 31727176⑈⑈

When someone writes a cheque, he or she can keep a record in the cheque book of what it was for and how much money was spent.

When a customer opens a current account, he or she usually receives a **cheque book** and a **debit card**. Every time the person uses the card or writes a **cheque**, he or she should keep a record of what has been spent. That way, the person will always know how much money is in the account.

Paying by cheque

Cheques have information printed on them. The account owner's name is on the cheque. The number of the cheque, the **account number**, and the number of the bank, or **sort code**, are printed at the bottom. The account number tells the bank who owns the **current account**.

This is what a cheque looks like.

Bank name

Account owner's name

Pearson Bank

Date _____

PAY THE
SUM OF _____

0981

£ _____

ROBERT J SMITH

Pearson Bank
PO Box 123, Jordan Court
Halley Hill, Oxford

⑈ 000981 ⑈   98-76-54⑆   10012345⑈

Cheque number

Account number

Sort code

The account owner has to fill in a cheque with certain information before any money can be paid to someone else.

Person or company being paid

Date

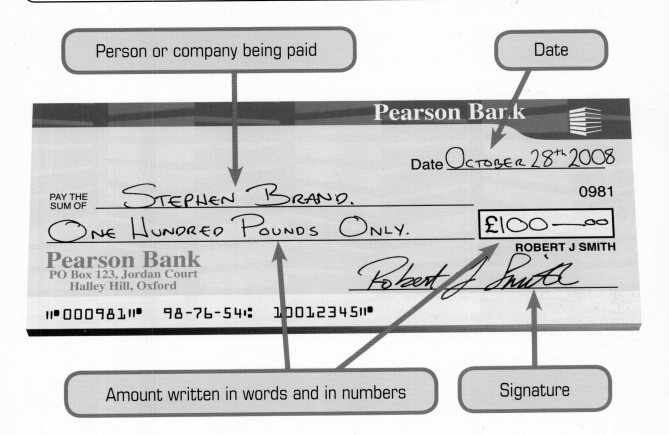

Amount written in words and in numbers

Signature

To use a cheque to pay money to someone else, the account owner must fill in the date, the name of the person who is to be paid, and how much the bank should pay that person. The account owner also has to put his or her signature at the bottom of the cheque.

What happens to a cheque?

Do you know what happens to a **cheque** after it is written? Here is the story of one cheque.

1. Said gets a cheque for £20 for his birthday from his aunt.

2. Said takes the cheque to the bank and pays it into his bank account.

3. The bank sends the cheque to the **clearinghouse** that keeps track of its business.

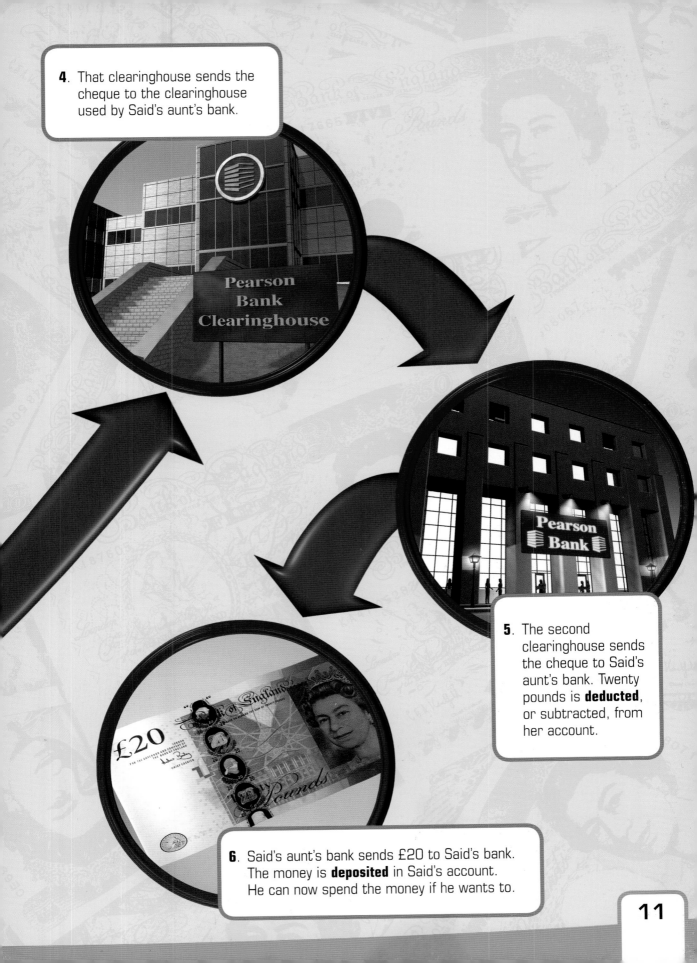

4. That clearinghouse sends the cheque to the clearinghouse used by Said's aunt's bank.

Pearson Bank Clearinghouse

Pearson Bank

5. The second clearinghouse sends the cheque to Said's aunt's bank. Twenty pounds is **deducted**, or subtracted, from her account.

£20

6. Said's aunt's bank sends £20 to Said's bank. The money is **deposited** in Said's account. He can now spend the money if he wants to.

Debit cards

Nowadays, people usually use the money in their **current account** without writing a cheque. They do this with a **debit card**. The numbers on the front of the card tell the bank what **account number** the card goes with. The card also has the account owner's name printed on the front. The owner must also put his or her signature on the back of the card.

Debit cards have the owner's signature on them and numbers that tell the bank who owns the account.

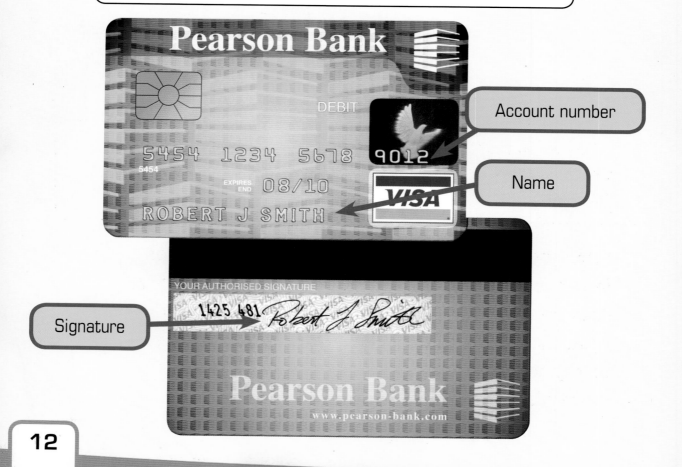

Account number

Name

Signature

```
25 MAR   S/O                       700.00-
25 MAR   POS                        21.12-
25 MAR   POS                        45.00-
25 MAR   POS                       438.60-
25 MAR   ATM                        40.00-
27 MAR   D/D                        27.11-

ACCOUNT           BALANCE      YOU CAN WITHDRAW
4430              £2787.40          £250


27/03/2008   10:57:26
```

CASHLINE

Thank you for using Cashline.

Keep Britain tidy

When people use their debit card to get money out of a **cashpoint machine**, they can get a slip of paper with a record of how much money has been taken out.

When people use a debit card, the money comes from their current account. Card owners must have enough money in their current account to pay for what they buy. A card owner should record debit card purchases to help keep track of how much money is in the account.

How debit cards work

Every **debit card** has a special chip in it. The chip has a code in it that gives the account number. The account owner puts the debit card into a special machine in a shop, called a **chip and pin machine**. This machine is linked to the bank's computers. It reads the code in the chip and deducts the money from the person's current account. The bank's computers send the money to the shop's bank account.

Chip and pin machines let shops and businesses check a customer's account information almost instantly.

Businesses must pay banks a **fee** every time a customer uses a debit card or **credit card** to pay for a purchase.

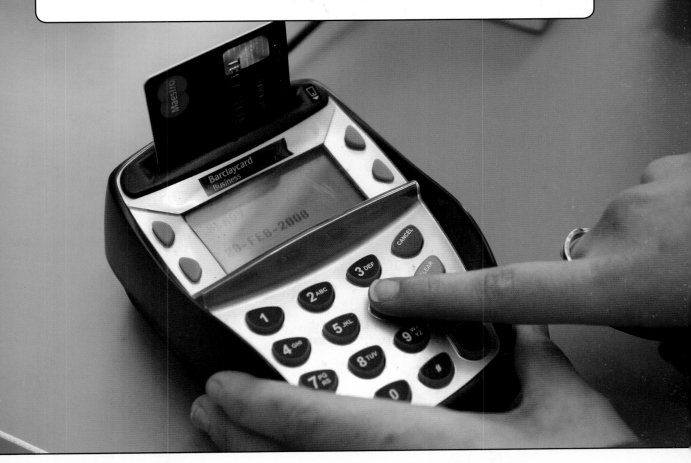

Usually, a person has to enter a **personal identification number (PIN)** into the chip and pin machine. Only the account owner should know the PIN. Sometimes, the customer must sign a **receipt** that the shop will keep. The customer will get a copy of the receipt that shows how much he or she spent.

Checking a current account

Every month, the bank makes a **bank statement** for each customer. It shows everything that happened with the person's account that month. It lists all the **cheques** that have been paid into and out of the account. It also lists purchases made with a **debit card**. These purchases are **deducted** from the person's **current account**.

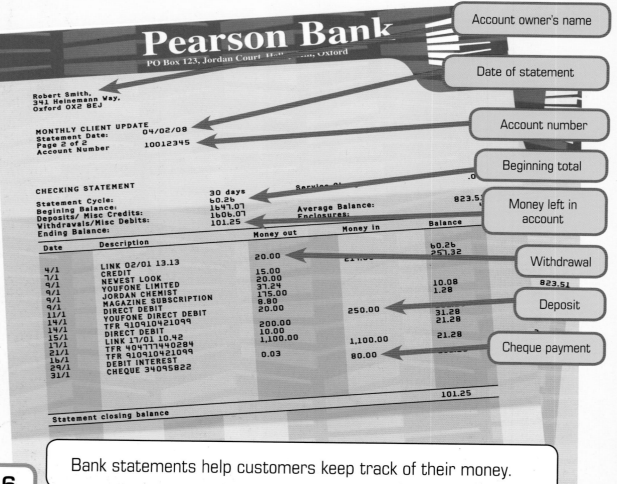

	Account owner's name
	Date of statement
	Account number
	Beginning total
	Money left in account
	Withdrawal
	Deposit
	Cheque payment

Pearson Bank
PO Box 123, Jordan Court Hall..... ....., Oxford

Robert Smith,
341 Heinemann Way,
Oxford OX2 8EJ

MONTHLY CLIENT UPDATE
Statement Date: 04/02/08
Page 2 of 2
Account Number   10012345

CHECKING STATEMENT

Statement Cycle:	30 days	Service ...		
Begining Balance:	60.26			823.5.
Deposits/ Misc Credits:	1647.07	Average Balance:		
Withdravals/Misc Debits:	1606.07	Enclosures:		
Ending Balance:	101.25			

Date	Description	Money out	Money in	Balance
				60.26
		20.00	21.00	257.32
4/1	LINK 02/01 13.13	15.00		
7/1	CREDIT	20.00		
9/1	NEWEST LOOK	37.24		10.08
9/1	YOUFONE LIMITED	175.00		1.28
9/1	JORDAN CHEMIST	8.80		
9/1	MAGAZINE SUBSCRIPTION	20.00	250.00	31.28
11/1	DIRECT DEBIT			21.28
14/1	YOUFONE DIRECT DEBIT	200.00		
14/1	TFR 910910421099	10.00		21.28
15/1	DIRECT DEBIT	1,100.00	1,100.00	
17/1	LINK 17/01 10.42			
21/1	TFR 404777440284	0.03	80.00	
16/1	TFR 910910421099			
29/1	DEBIT INTEREST			
31/1	CHEQUE 34095822			
				101.25

Statement closing balance

823.51

Bank statements help customers keep track of their money.

The bank statement shows every **deposit** made to the current account, too. These are added to the account. The statement shows how much money is still in the current account. It is important to check a bank statement carefully, to be sure there are no mistakes.

Account owners should check that their bank statements match their own records. If someone else has been taking money out of the account, it is important to find this out quickly and stop it.

Buy now and pay later

People can buy things without using **cash**, **cheques**, or **debit cards**. They can buy things even when they do not have the money to pay for them straightaway. Buying things this way is called buying on **credit**. It is like getting a **loan**. The money has to be paid back later.

To get a credit card or loan, a person must have a record showing that he or she pays bills on time.

SOFA SO GOOD!

BUY NOW PAY LATER

So why wait ... come and visit!

36 months free credit !!!

OPEN 7 DAYS A WEEK · FREE PARKING

Banks and credit card companies offer different kinds of credit cards to customers.

To buy things on credit, people use another special card called a **credit card**. Every credit card has a **credit limit**. This is the greatest amount of money a person can spend using the card. The person has to pay some money to the credit card company every month to be allowed to keep using the card.

Credit cards

Many banks give **credit cards** to their customers. There are also credit card companies, shops, and other businesses that offer cards. A credit card looks like a **debit card**. On the front it has the name of the bank or credit card company, a special **account number**, and the customer's name. On the back it has a magnetic strip and the account owner's signature.

> Credit cards and debit cards have a **security code** inside the signature box. This code is often used to make **online** purchases.

Chip

Account number

Magnetic strip

Signature

Security code

If a debit card or credit card gets lost or stolen, the bank or credit card company must be told straightaway. That way, the card can be cancelled so that nobody else can use it. It is important to keep track of **bank cards**.

Card owners must report lost credit cards to the bank or credit card company straightaway.

How credit cards work

Like a **debit card**, a **credit card** goes into a **chip and pin machine** in a shop. This machine is linked to the bank's computers. The card owner enters a **personal identification number (PIN)** into the chip and pin machine. The customer then gets a **receipt** for his or her records.

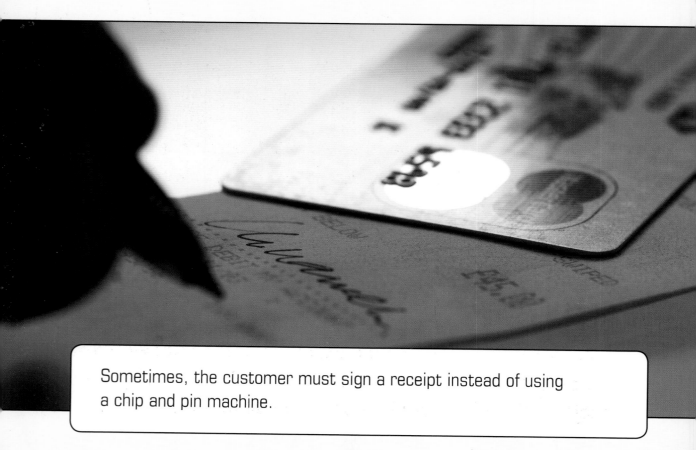

Sometimes, the customer must sign a receipt instead of using a chip and pin machine.

Many people use credit cards to buy things on the **Internet**. It is important to check that the website is safe and the credit card details will be kept secret.

The credit card owner gets a bill every month. The bill lists all the purchases the card owner has made with the credit card. The owner must check the bill carefully to make sure that he or she has made all the payments.

Interest

A **credit card** owner can pay the whole bill at once or just part of it. The amount paid straightaway is the payment. The amount left over is the **balance**. The balance is a **loan**.

Many people write a **cheque** to pay their credit card bill.

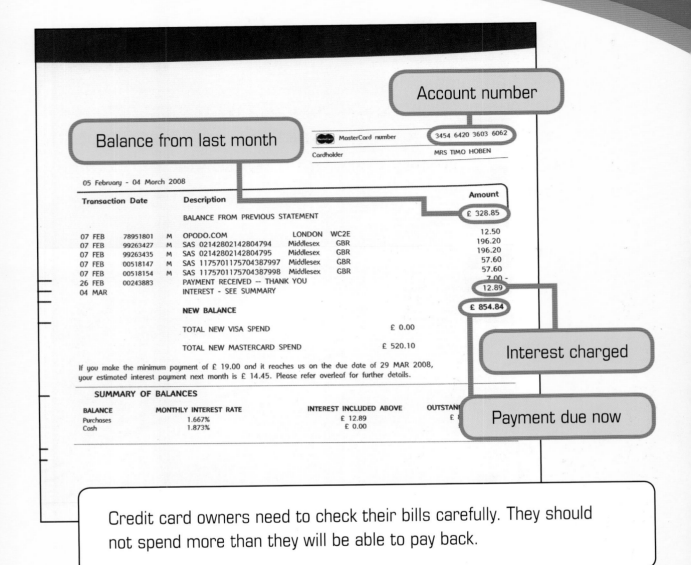

Account number

Balance from last month

MasterCard number   3454 6420 3603 6062

Cardholder   MRS TIMO HOBEN

05 February - 04 March 2008

Transaction Date			Description			Amount
			BALANCE FROM PREVIOUS STATEMENT			£ 328.85
07 FEB	78951801	M	OPODO.COM	LONDON	WC2E	12.50
07 FEB	99263427	M	SAS 02142802142804794	Middlesex	GBR	196.20
07 FEB	99263435	M	SAS 02142802142804795	Middlesex	GBR	196.20
07 FEB	00518147	M	SAS 1175701175704387997	Middlesex	GBR	57.60
07 FEB	00518154	M	SAS 1175701175704387998	Middlesex	GBR	57.60
26 FEB	00243883		PAYMENT RECEIVED -- THANK YOU			7.00 -
04 MAR			INTEREST - SEE SUMMARY			12.89

NEW BALANCE £ 854.84

TOTAL NEW VISA SPEND   £ 0.00

TOTAL NEW MASTERCARD SPEND   £ 520.10

Interest charged

If you make the minimum payment of £ 19.00 and it reaches us on the due date of 29 MAR 2008, your estimated interest payment next month is £ 14.45. Please refer overleaf for further details.

SUMMARY OF BALANCES

BALANCE	MONTHLY INTEREST RATE	INTEREST INCLUDED ABOVE	OUTSTAN
Purchases	1.667%	£ 12.89	£
Cash	1.873%	£ 0.00	

Payment due now

Credit card owners need to check their bills carefully. They should not spend more than they will be able to pay back.

The bank or credit card company lets the account owner borrow the money, but it charges a **fee** for this service. This fee is called **interest**, and it is added to the person's next bill. The longer it takes to pay a bill completely, the more interest the person will end up paying. So, it is a good idea to pay the total amount of the bill as quickly as possible.

Debt

A **debt** is money owed to someone. A **credit card balance** is a kind of debt. There are other types of debt. Most people do not have enough money to pay for a house, car, or university education all at once. They borrow money from a bank or **loan** company.

Many people use loans to help them study. They will have to pay the loans back when they have a job.

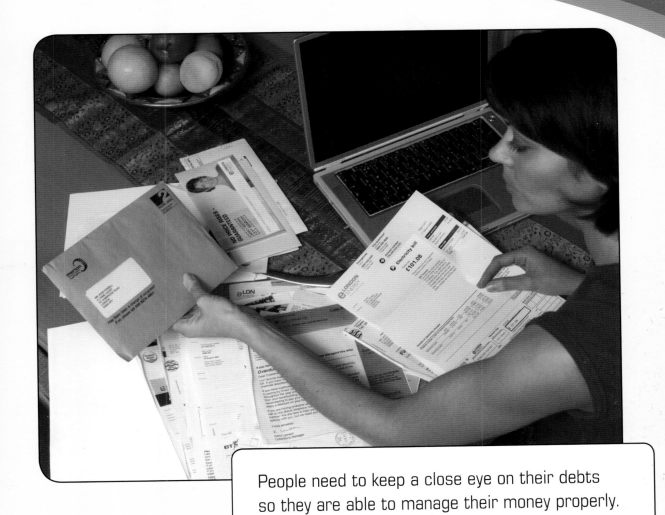

People need to keep a close eye on their debts so they are able to manage their money properly.

Like any other debt, credit card debt must be paid back. The money does not have to be paid all at once. However, **interest** is added to the amount owed. The longer it takes to pay back, the more interest is charged. Interest adds up quickly. It makes debts harder to pay back. So, it is important to use credit cards carefully.

Using credit wisely

One way to use **credit** wisely is not to use it too often. Another is to pay **credit card debts** quickly. Everyone has certain needs. Food, clothes, transport, and a place to live are all examples of things people must pay for.

Families usually spend a large amount of their money on food.

Wants are things like holidays, expensive cars, and restaurant meals.

Everyone also has wants. Wants are things people would like to have, but could do without. People should think carefully about what they buy so they do not get into debt for things they do not really need. It is important to make wise choices about how to spend money.

Glossary

account number number that tells who a bank account belongs to

balance amount of money still owed

bank card plastic card given to a customer by a bank to buy things without using cash

bank statement record of what happens to the money a person keeps in the bank

cash coins and paper money

cashpoint machine machine that lets people use bank services without seeing a cashier

cheque note from the owner of a bank account telling the bank to pay money from the account to someone

cheque book booklet of cheques

chip and pin machine machine that reads credit and debit cards

clearinghouse business that helps a bank take care of its money

credit borrowed money

credit card thin, plastic bank card that lets someone buy something and pay for it later

credit limit total amount of money a person can borrow

current account service offered by a bank that lets people use their money without carrying cash

debit card thin, plastic card, used instead of a cheque, that lets someone pay for something using money from their current account

debt money owed to someone

deduct to take away or subtract

deposit money put into a bank account. Or to put money into a bank account.

fee money charged for a service

interest money charged for borrowing money. Or money paid to people for letting the bank use their money to run its business.

Internet network of computers around the world through which information is shared

loan money someone borrows

online connected to the Internet

personal identification number (PIN) secret number used with debit cards and credit cards, which only the account owner knows. It is used to get money at cashpoints and to buy goods and services.

receipt record showing the amount of a transaction or how much someone spent

security code numbers found inside the signature box of a bank card that are used as an extra safety measure for online purchases

service something done for someone

sort code code that gives the address of the card owner's bank

Index